SACRED ANGELS

Coloring Experiences for the Mystical and Magical

Illustrations by
Lydia Hess

HARPER**ELIXIR**
An Imprint of HarperCollinsPublishers

This book is dedicated to my family.
My husband, Robbie, for his
steadfast support and encouragement;
my daughters, Tucker and Aubrey,
for their creative ideas and consultation.

HarperCollins books may be purchased for educational, business, or sales promotional use. For information please e-mail the Special Markets Department at SPsales@harpercollins.com.

HarperCollins website: http://www.harpercollins.com

FIRST EDITION
Designed by Lydia Hess
Library of Congress Cataloging-in-Publication Data is available upon request.
ISBN 978–0–06–256365–1

16 17 18 19 20 BRR 10 9 8 7 6 5 4 3 2 1

Welcome to *Sacred Angels*. As you set out on a journey of inspiration that bridges worlds both within and without, we invite you to contemplate the benevolent essence embodied in these images. Across millennia and wisdom traditions our ancestors have told of otherworldly messengers, light beings that deliver divine truths and offer compassionate guidance and loving guardianship. These ethereal presences awaken in us a sense of all that is graceful, merciful, beautiful, and enduring. Our hope is that as you color, your mind quiets and your everyday cares recede as your soul expands.

LYDIA HESS

ETERNITY

HEAVENS

LYDIA HESS

PROTECTION

[Archangel Michael]

KINDNESS

GUIDANCE

[Archangel Gabriel]

BLESSING

RENEWAL

[Archangel Raphael]

SANCTUARY

ILLUMINATION

[Archangel Jophiel]

PURITY

WISDOM

[Archangel Uriel]

MERCY

ARDOR

[*Psyche and Cupid*]

GRACE

LOVE

LYDIA HESS

DEVOTION

INTIMACY

CONNECTION

DESTINY

[Masleh Zodiac Angel]

LYDIA HESS

JOY

GENTLENESS

HARMONY

TENDERNESS

DELIGHT

ABUNDANCE

DIVINITY

PEACE

SERENITY

AMITY

PROSPERITY

PASSION

VITALITY

CLARITY

[Frida Angel]

TRANQUILITY

TRANSCENDENCE

INTUITION

UNITY

HOPE

THE
END